© 1994 Watts Books

Watts Books
96 Leonard Street
London
EC2A 4RH

Franklin Watts Australia
14 Mars Road
Lane Cove
NSW 2066

UK ISBN: 0 7496 1531 1

Dewey Decimal Classification Number 728

10 9 8 7 6 5 4 3 2 1

A CIP catalogue record for this book is
available from the British Library.

Editor: Sarah Ridley
Designer: Janet Watson
Picture researcher: Sarah Moule
Illustrators: Robert and Rhoda Burns

Photographs: Eye Ubiquitous 5, 21, 26;
Image Bank 24; Robert Harding Picture
Library cover, 12, 23; Telegraph Colour
Library 11, 15; Tony Stone Worldwide 6,
16, 18, 28; ZEFA 9.

Printed in Malaysia

LIFT OFF!

SKYSCRAPERS

Joy Richardson

WATTS BOOKS
London • New York • Sydney

Space in the sky

Many cities are short of space.
There is not enough room for everyone
to live and work at ground level.

Skyscrapers save space.
They are cheaper to build
than several separate buildings.
They make it possible for lots of people
to work together in the same place.

New York is built on an island.
Skyscrapers soar upwards,
making the most of space on the ground.

Building tall

In the past, it was difficult to make buildings more than a few storeys high.

Castles and cathedrals had to have very thick walls to support the weight of the building and keep it from collapsing.

The Leaning Tower of Pisa was built about eight hundred years ago. The ground beneath it was rather soft. The heavy weight of stone made the eight storey tower begin to sink and lean over to one side.

Firm foundations

Tall buildings need strong foundations.

Skyscrapers stand on concrete piles
which are like roots in the ground.
The piles are driven down through
the earth to solid rock below.

New York stands on hard rock which
makes a good support for skyscrapers.

In cities like London, the ground is soft.
Sometimes builders have to dig
a huge hole and fill it with concrete.
This makes a giant platform
for the skyscraper to stand on.

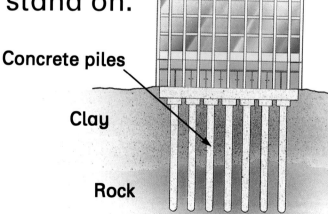

Concrete piles

Clay

Rock

Working with metal

Old buildings carried all
the weight on their walls which
pressed down on the foundations.

Then iron and steel came into use.
Iron was very strong, but
lighter to use than brick or stone.
Steel was even stronger.

Buildings could now be made with
a metal skeleton to carry the weight.

Just over a hundred years ago,
the Eiffel Tower was built in Paris.
This metal framework was 300 metres high.
It was the tallest structure in the world.

A strong frame

Metal frames made skyscrapers possible.

The first metal-framed skyscraper
was built in 1885, in Chicago.
It was ten storeys tall.

Inside a skyscraper, the
metal frame supports
all the weight of roofs and floors,
walls and windows, people and furniture.

This framework is made from
steel bars called girders which
are lifted into place with cranes.
The girders are bolted together, or
welded so that the ends join up.

A concrete middle

Skyscrapers are made mainly of
metal and reinforced concrete.
Reinforced concrete is concrete with
steel bars running through it.
It is a very strong building material
which can carry a lot of weight.

Some skyscrapers are built around
a tall tube of reinforced concrete.
This tube goes right up through
the middle of the building.

Floor beams branch out from the tube.
Wires, pipes and lifts can run
up and down inside it.

Skyscraper skin

When the framework is complete,
concrete floors are lifted up
or made on each level.

Outside walls are attached like skin
to the skeleton frame of the skyscraper.
This outer skin is called cladding.

Cladding panels are made in factories.
They are lifted into place and
fitted to the framework.

The Empire State Building is clad
with panels of limestone and granite.
The heavy cladding keeps it
from swaying in the wind.

Giant walls

Cladding panels can be made of stone, concrete, aluminium or glass.

The cladding can be light and thin but it must be windproof and watertight.

Hundreds or even thousands of windows are set into the cladding. The lines of windows make patterns on the skyscraper walls.

Some skyscrapers are smoothly clad from top to bottom with tinted glass which reflects the sky and the streets.

Open underneath

Skyscraper foundations
support the framework.
This means that the walls
do not have to touch the ground.

Some skyscrapers stand up on stilts.
The Hong Kong and Shanghai Bank
has an open space beneath it.

Some skyscrapers stand in
a deep hole in the ground.
Underground basements can be
used for car parking or storage.

Life inside

Inside the skyscraper, walls are fitted to make separate rooms.

Heating, water, electricity and telephones are needed at every level. Pipes and cables are laid in spaces between each floor and the ceiling below.

Lifts are installed to carry people speedily up and down.

The top of the skyscraper may be used for gardens or a helicopter pad. It may carry a television mast, or lights to warn aircraft.

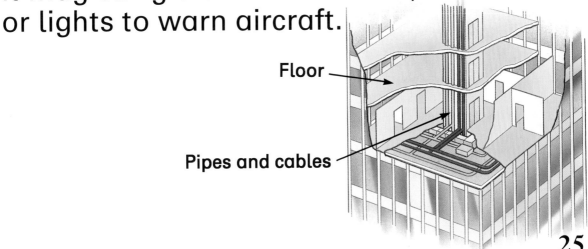

Floor

Pipes and cables

City skyline

Architects can make skyscrapers
square, round, triangular or many-sided,
with flat tops or pointed tops.

Each design must be tested for strength
before it is built, to make sure it will
not sway too far in the wind.

Architects keep working to find ways
of making skyscrapers taller,
stronger or better looking.

As new skyscrapers reach
into the sky in crowded cities,
the skyline keeps changing.

The sky is the limit

The ten tallest skyscrapers
are all in America.

The tallest building in the world
is the Sears Tower in Chicago.
It is 443 metres tall and has 110 storeys.
There are 104 lifts and 16,100 windows.
17,000 people work in the building.

There are plans in Japan to build
a skyscraper twice as tall as that.

Index